INVESTING
for
BEGINNERS

INVESTING
for
BEGINNERS

KEVIN T MUIR

Library of Congress Control Number: 2022909208
ISBN: Hardcover   978-1-6698-8873-4
                Softcover   978-1-6698-8872-7
                eBook   978-1-6698-8871-0

Print information available on the last page.

Rev. date: 07/07/2022

To order additional copies of this book, contact:
Xlibris
AU TFN: 1 800 844 927 (Toll Free inside Australia)
AU Local: (02) 8310 8187 (+61 2 8310 8187 from outside Australia)
www.Xlibris.com.au
Orders@Xlibris.com.au
837997

CONTENTS

About the Author xi

Preface xix

Easy Come, Easy Go xxix

Investing For Beginners 1

Self-Managed Super Fund (SMSF) 21

Franked Dividends 23

Winners and Losers 25

Diversification 31

PE Ratio 35

Capital Gains Tax is Not Lost Money 47

FOMO – Fear of Missing Out 49

MONEY

MONEY

MONEY

IT'S A RICH MAN'S WORLD

INVESTING for BEGINNERS

KEVIN T MUIR
2021

I feel that this book should be directed primarily at people who have recently left school or university and are about to start their first job and collect their first pay cheque.

There is so much temptation out there that it doesn't take long for young people to want to try and buy all the exciting things they never could afford at school. And because credit is so easy to get, it's not long before they find themselves in debt. If they pay off the debt, then okay, but what happens is debt becomes a habit.

This book tries to steer them away from debt and get them into a savings and investment habit.

ABOUT THE AUTHOR

Kevin Muir lives on the Gold Coast overlooking miles of beautiful sandy beaches. Although not a professional share trader, he now owns a substantial quantity of big four bank shares, which allows him to lead a dream life of camper-vanning, surfing, golfing, and writing.

Kevin experienced the market crash in the'60s, the'74 crash, the'87 crash, the '92 crash, the 2008 crash, and the 2020 pandemic crash. What he learnt—the hard way—is in this book.

Kevin also remembers well when the Commonwealth Bank made its initial public offering (IPO) at a price of $5.40. Kevin had sold his business and was in a position to be able to purchase 500,000 CBA shares.

Kevin bought industrial property instead. Why? Kevin new nothing about the share market other than it's a place where people seem to lose most of their money. Nowhere could he find genuine information about how the stock exchange and the share market worked. Nor did he have faith in advice he received from so-called financial advisers, who seemed more interested in pointing him to investments where the adviser got the highest commission, rather than being able to satisfy Kevin's request for IPO investment advice.

Those CBA shares today are worth $50 million and the industrial property about $5 million.

Kevin is convinced that there is a lot of young people out there who have no clue about how the stock exchange and share market operates.

They only know people lose money, their only source of information being the media.

After 15 years of being involved in the Australian share market, Kevin knows success— and he sure knows the pitfalls.

Young people have plenty of access to books from successful investors on what to do but very little genuine information on what NOT to do when it comes to investing.

Kevin's book explains how the share market works, but more importantly, it provides young people with real-time advice to stop them from making investment mistakes and also points out how ridiculous it is for young people to rely on others to organise their retirement income.

This book shows every young person how to get their act together so as to retire earlier without lowering their expected standard of living.

Do not invest without absorbing every page in this book—Kevin's first and best advice for every novice investor.

SOMEWHERE ON THE HIGH MISTY PLATEAU IN FAR NORTH KENYA, A LION SHAKES ITSELF AWAKE AND BEING HUNGRY, WONDERS IF TODAY IT MIGHT CATCH THE SLOWEST GAZELLE.

ON THE SAME MORNING, IN THE SAME MIST, A SLEEPY GAZELLE WAKES ITSELF UP AND IMMEDIATELY HOPES THAT TODAY IT CAN OUTRUN THE FASTEST LION ONCE AGAIN. [original source unknown]

IN THE MEANTIME, BACK IN THE SUBURBS, THE MORTGAGE HAS TO BE PAID, THE RATES ARE DUE SOON, THE KIDS' SCHOOL FEES NEED TO BE EARNED, THE SUV NEEDS A *100,000* SERVICE, AND THE MOTHER-IN-LAW ARRIVES TOMORROW.

JUST ANOTHER DAY . . .

TOMORROW'S PROBABLY THE SAME—AND THE NEXT DAY.

UNLESS YOU DECIDE OTHERWISE?

Hi, Dear Reader,

If you are about to start reading this book, then you're probably thinking seriously about how to be financially successful. That's good.

As you read, you will see that to be successful takes sustainable planning. It also takes severe discipline, plus good judgement. Planning and good judgement are in this book; the discipline part—well, that's up to you.

It's a fact of life that you can and will learn a lot more from your mistakes than you will learn from your successes. But unfortunately, making mistakes is expensive, it's time-consuming, and it's a killer of enthusiasm.

Consequently, we need to avoid making our own mistakes and learn from other people's mistakes!

In other words, take a shortcut to success.

That's where this book excels!

Part of this book shows you one safe plan to reach your financial goal, but the bulk of the book points out something more important, something more essential to becoming successful.

The book spends a lot of pages pointing out to you, dear reader, WHAT NOT TO INVEST IN.

Knowing what to stay well clear of is just as important as knowing what to invest in.

As you read and absorb, make sure that what I advise you to have NOTHING TO DO WITH, gets firmly fixed in your mind, as there are millions of so-called financial wizards out there in 'money-land'—all falling over themselves—to pass on to you 'their expertise' on how to make you 'successful'!

Unfortunately, their idea of success is to turn a good percentage of your money into their money.

This book is all the information you need to NOT make investment mistakes.

Read and learn . . .

> *Ordinary people are not destined to be rich.*
> *They have to plan and execute.*

CAUTION

DO *NOT* read every section in one reading session—*you will suffer 'information overload', causing you to not absorb important information.*

PREFACE

'Trading shares' on the ASX is dangerously exciting as opposed to 'investing' on the ASX, which is not so exciting.

'Trading' is simply gambling on an estimated outcome. For example, you purchase shares because your crystal ball says the shares will go up in value.

'Investing', on the other hand, is buying excellent quality dividend-paying shares and holding on to them over several years.

Unfortunately, 99% of newcomers to the share market arrive with the attitude that buying and selling shares is the only way to make serious cash.

This book is all about what NOT to do if you have money to invest. But first, there is some valuable information to be learnt.

Knowing this information and then never forgetting it will definitely save you a lot of angst (and money).

If you flip a coin three times, and each time it comes up heads, you would then be fairly certain the next flip would be tails. If the next flip comes up heads again (four in a row!), then you can be absolutely dead certain the next flip will be tails.

Does that sound familiar? Yes. Unfortunately, it's human nature to think like that. But it's an absolutely useless human trait AND fatal as far as the share market is concerned.

The first flip of your coin has absolutely NO *connection to the next flip of your coin or the previous flips of the same coin for that matter. Each flip is totally unconnected to any other flip.*

Regardless of your opinion, there is no reason not to get five or ten heads in a row.

Okay, this is the information you need to know: Whatever reason you have for buying or selling certain shares has absolutely no connection to what will happen next to these same shares.

It's simple: Whatever you think will happen in the market will not happen!

You need to be aware that at any one time, 3 billion people from all over the world have access to the share market. Your buying of a share because you think it will increase in value could, within a nanosecond, be sold by a person on the other side of the world who knows the shares will lose value.

Like flipping coins, buying shares because of what you think will happen or should happen is pointless. Thinking a share will increase in value is exactly the same as tossing a coin—the outcome is absolutely unpredictable.

Because there is definitely no apparent logic in why the market moves, hoping for a good result from your transaction, buying, selling, or flipping is simply gambling; it's not investing.

Consequently, how successful you become as an investor depends on your understanding of the above information.

And on another issue, which will decide how good an investor you are or think you are, it's definitely NOT *on what you do when the market is trading 'normally' but what you do when the market is in 'freefall' and panic is pandemic!*

This 'freefall' situation separates the boys from the men!

Believe me, panic-selling happens, and it's frightening. But it can also be profitable if you are aware of how people react to market drama.

Okay, enough said, now read on and absorb.

INVESTING *in most cases is mainly to provide income and also capital gain. But at the end of the day (read: retirement time),* INCOME *is basically the real reason for saving and investing.*

What's generally not understood, though, is that to end up with income at retirement time takes more than just investing.

On day 1, you need to take charge of three scenarios.

First is to work on increasing your monthly salary.

This 'increasing your monthly salary' could be worked on over your working life, for instance, by becoming more qualified (read: MBA) or raising yourself up through the ranks to managerial levels, etc.

Second, as soon as you start your working life, you need to develop a very serious spending/savings BUDGET.

It has to be a budget that allows you to actually have money left over from living expenses, in other words surplus money, money solely for your future lifestyle.

This saving of surplus money, during the very early years of your working life, is actually the important key to being successful financially in the later part of your life.

Understand this: Your very first $5,000 saved can, over your working life, become $320,000. (Good quality investments generally double every seven years. I'll let you join the dots!)

Of course, the discipline that leads to having surplus money is really the holy grail of this future success.

There is no savings without discipline.

Unfortunately, the early years of your working life are the most challenging, especially for young people fresh into the workforce, as there's heaps of social distractions out there, all with one purpose—to make sure you have fun!

Fun and good times are not free.

However, once we get the hang of actually having funds to spare at the end of each week, trust me, it won't be long before you will start to see a flicker of light at the end of the tunnel.

Of course, now that we have spare funds accumulating in our savings account, we need to consider doing something serious with these funds.

So the third option then is to start considering what to invest our hard-earned savings in.

It being hard-earned and you making huge personal sacrifices along the way (to eventually have savings) means investing has got to be a serious decision!

And when the going gets tough, try and remember, tough doesn't last! What actually happens is that in time, your investment will start to outperform your savings habit. That day is unbelievably exhilarating—you've actually outsmarted the system!

But to get this far, for a long time, it's going to be 50% savings/ discipline and 50% sensible investing. You can't have one without the other. It just won't work!

It's one of the most important lessons you can learn.

So what do we need to do to get your savings earning their keep?

Well, that's where this book starts earning its keep!

If you're still reading this book, it means you're curious, which is a good sign, but if you're reading only to see if there's an easy way to get from zilch too mega rich, that's not so good! It indicates you're a bit of a slow learner. Re-read the first pages again—NO easy money! If you can't get that into your head, then you're the dude who's going to be washing my Porsche!

However, regardless of your intentions, the show continues.

Investing for beginners is the next section. It contains info you cannot bypass—it's the key for your rags-to-riches adventure.

Of course, before you get to the nitty-gritty of successful investing, we have a small mountain to scale.

It's called a job! (Actually, occupation *or* career *sounds better.)*

We need a job to get some loot to turn into more loot.

If you've been working after school, or during the school holidays, you'll have a rough idea of how work is not all it's cracked up to be: long hours, odd hours, crappy boss. Or if you've been lucky, maybe your job was exciting, good pay, nice boss, but I suspect that's the exception.

Bottom line, though, is your work produced INCOME, *which you've probably spent or saved to spend later.*

And income is what work's all about—excitement and satisfaction are ranked second; INCOME *is first!*

Deciding on a job may seem a very big decision. Your parents will convince you of that as they will be of the old school, which means your job selection should be secure and permanent—read 'for life'.

That thinking is yesterday! You and your friends are definitely not going to be doing the same thing for the rest of your working days—too boring for a start. Plus, how can you become a confident experienced worldly person by doing the same thing day after day? It's not going to happen.

Object one of job search: Find the job that pays you the most money. Keep in mind that you're not much value to any bosses at this early stage in your working adventure.

Of course, the job or career that you think you're destined for may not be the highest-paying job you could score. So you may have to back track into some job that pays more but lacks excitement. So be it! We are not going to be doing it for life.

Actually, the only reasons we are getting a job are, one, definitely for the money, two, your parents are sick of supporting you, and three, to get work experience.

And work experience includes the following—so get used to it.

It comes as a shock to some young teenagers that, all of a sudden, someone with real authority is bossing them around—kicking arse, in other words!

And you thought your parents were strict!

Like I said, better get used to it—Mum's not going to be around to pick up after you! But at least console yourself with the thought that someday you'll do the kicking—but only if you play your cards right.

How much you are going to get paid? For the rest of your working life, income depends on two things: qualifications and ability.

Unfortunately, in your case, when applying for your first serious job, the only thing taken into consideration is 'qualifications'. Ability counts for zilch, even though you think you are the hottest thing since Steve Jobs. Your new boss has no idea of your ability. He can only judge you on how well you have done at school or university. If he employs you, he will be hoping like hell you actually do have ability like our friend Steve.

Bottom line: Qualifications are all that matter. Don't leave school or university too early, get qualified, unless you're happy washing cars . . . forever!

Want to increase your income even more? Keep getting more qualifications, keep searching for more experience.

You can actually talk your way into a job. But if you talk the talk, you better be able to walk the walk. Or you'll definitely be walking.

Leaving a job for better pay or experience is one thing, which you should not hesitate to do, but getting fired is something else. It will affect your future prospects, and it could affect your credit rating.

So it's simple: Don't get fired!

Actually, from here on, make sure you THINK *before you do anything stupid! Jumping off a roof into a shallow swim pool—not smart. Doing burnouts, drink driving—not smart. Getting drunk, reckless sex—not smart. Picking a fight with Mister Unknown—not smart. Showing the world how dumb you are but opening your mouth—not smart either. Best to work on keeping your act together. You can still have fun if you've got great friends. As for bad friends, simple: Delete them.*

And whilst you're at it, always take stock by asking yourself, how valuable am I to my friends or the company? Am I an asset? Do I make money for the owners? Am I worth more? Am I getting ahead?

And an even more important question: Who or what is holding me back from getting ahead? Hopefully, not yourself. Always dress properly, or dress like a boss. Someone higher up will notice.

Okay, enough said. On with the show, and good luck with job-seeking. Extreme frustration will be your constant companion, but a job is not your right—it's a privilege. No one is obligated to provide you with a job. Just because you are you, it doesn't mean that bosses will fall over themselves to hire you.

When you finally do crack it for a job, don't blow it. As this is your first serious chance to raise yourself above the mob.

Next on the agenda is pay day. With pay day will come decisions. You need to decide asap whether you are a consumer or a saver.

Dead set, you are now at the fork in the road.

Consumers are spenders. They buy stuff that always loose value: cars, jet skis, TVs, clothes, shoes, bags, holidays, bikes, gym gear, etc. But the dumbest consumer is the one that borrows to buy the stuff; only surpassed, of course, by an even dumber person—one who buys stuff just to give the impression that they are successful. Wow! Staying broke pretending to be rich! So much for consumers!

On the other hand, successful people buy stuff that go up in value: blue-chip shares, waterfront properties, start-up companies with excellent prospects, start your own business etc.

Pretty obvious, isn't it? Discipline *is the key word here. It's your decision.*

Okay, I hope you've got your head around all the above info. Yes? Okay, continue.

EASY COME, EASY GO . . .

No saying is more true, when it comes to people who have inherited money or people who have accidently picked the six lotto numbers . . .

A hardworking family I knew actually won lotto, which back then was a little over a million dollars—enough to retire on quite comfortably. There were three teenage kids in the family, so the old man bought each of the kids a brand new car and then bought Mum a new car. He also bought a new work vehicle for himself. With what was left over, the old man bought a small industrial shed as a depot to work his business out of.

Twenty-two years later, Dad is still working. The cars are long gone, and the industrial building, to make it sellable or rentable, requires extensive renovation—with money they don't have.

Twenty-two years ago, Mum and Dad could have retired very comfortably. The one million sensibly invested would have at least doubled every seven years to about eight million today.

Makes you wonder, doesn't it?

It's just so easy to make the wrong decision.

*   *   *

Another example of your everyday mum and dad investor . . .

Recently, some people inherited a lot of money from a deceased estate property sale. Granma died.

They were bubbling with excitement (who could blame them?) when they ask me what I thought they should do with the money.

They were thinking waterfront property with a mooring and a 40-foot Riviera sports cruiser. I was thinking that they actually had enough to retire on if it was properly invested in dividend-paying shares.

So I suggested bank shares, CBA actually, as the share price was quite low compared to normal. Consequently, the dividend was about 9%, relative to its share price.

No possible way did they want anything to do with the share market. The share market is where people lose their money! And banks can go broke!

A year later, I crossed their path. Naturally, I asked them what they did with the money: bought a boat and put the balance into a savings deposit at 1.75% p.a.

Which bank? CBA, of course. (These are the same people who told me banks could go broke!)

The $850,000 they inherited immediately invested in CBA shares would have paid them $76,000 in dividends, and the 12-month capital gain from the share price increase would have increased their wealth by another $120,000 ($192,000 in total).

However, the sad truth is that their $400,000 boat has lost about $50,000 in value, and the interest on the term deposit amounted to $7,875.

Instead of increasing their capital to $192,000, they have actually now lost $42,125 from their capital and still working.

You can join the dots.

Actually, the dumb investment list is endless—just make sure you're not on it!

A wise man does not hoard money; inflation will erode it away. Instead, a wise man invests in two areas: income-producing investments or investments with capital gain.

INVESTING FOR BEGINNERS

It is an indictment on the population of Australia, that with all the saving options and generous tax deduction advantages, plus endless government encouragement and superannuation copayments by employers to employees, negative gearing, term deposits, share market investments, ONLY 3% of the population at age 70 is in a position to retire on a comfortable self-funded retirement income.

That is only 3% of us do not need to rely on government assistance via a government aged pension.

It's just so hard to believe that only 3% of us have the planning ability and the necessary discipline that's required to NOT end up relying on a government aged pension when we reach retirement age.

But it's true!

And bear in mind, any retirement income that is LESS than your combined (husband and wife) working income will mean that you will have to lower your standard of living, which is not a very attractive option as you enter what should be the best years of your life.

Wasn't the idea of working and slaving away 50 years of your life all about being able to knock off the ball and chain and then start living the dream?

Mind you, 25% of the workforce are totally convinced that the government actually owes them an aged pension—and a comfortable one at that!

With their head in the sand, it hasn't dawned on them (until it's too late) that the remuneration (read: pension) is a lot less than the average working wage—the same working wage that they were complaining about, it not being enough to make ends meet. Yet they are quite happy to settle for a future pension that definitely won't be enough to make ends meet!

Believe me—you DO NOT want to arrive at retirement age and then have to scrimp and save just to pay the electricity bill.

But KEEP SPENDING and FAIL TO PLAN, and eventually, to your amazement and disappointment, in retirement, you will be struggling just to pay the registration on your worn-out vehicle! Not what you had in mind? What makes you any different from the other 97% of the workforce?

The fact of the matter is you just cannot retire in comfort by relying on financial institutions or on employer contributions or by saving only 5% of your income. At best you might end up at age 65 with a house that may be freehold but is in need of a renovation and is surrounded by other older properties in need of renovations, or a home that still needs paying off and, if you're very lucky, an income from your super fund of about 25% or less of your working income, or only the dreaded pension!

You should not *be okay with any of the above scenarios.*

The other more serious fact of the matter is you only get one chance to accumulate serious retirement income, and it takes a whole working life to do this. You can't get to age 65 and find out that you are short of funds so you decide to do another 50 years of work.

It's too late—you're at the end of the road.

You'll survive, but it won't be a life sailing around the Greek islands!

It also never fails to amaze me the number of people who are working to pay off the home mortgage with the intent that come retirement time, they will sell the house, buy a smaller beach side place, in other words downsize, and use the difference in money to retire in comfort, spending the rest of their days walking in the sun along the beach.

Trust me, that scenario is NOT planning for retirement. The difference in the selling price of your old place and the cost of your downsized property will not leave enough money to retire on. It will be just enough money left over to prevent you from getting the aged pension.

Rather than use the glamorous word 'downsize', try using 'downgrade' instead because that's what it will be.

By now, you should be starting to question whether you are on track to a nice comfortable retirement or whether you really need to get your act together before you pass the point of no return.

Remember, it takes nearly every successful retiree a lifetime of careful financial control to reach the goal of financial security that will be comfortable and last you the 20 or 30 years of your expected retirement.

If you're 20, great. There's hope. If you're 40 and you've done nothing serious towards financial freedom, then it's going to be difficult. If you're 60 with nothing in the kitty, get used to scrimping and saving.

Okay, so you now have decided you definitely need to do something constructive financially to get your potential retirement income on track so that the result is an income that provides the sort of money you estimate you'll need to keep the style of living you hope to become accustomed to.

The very first lesson is the hardest lesson to get through to people: There is NO fast money. There is no quick way to accumulate funds.

Even people lucky enough to win the lottery end up back where they started after a few years! Easy come, easy go!

The longer it takes to accumulate funds, and the more sacrifices you make, the more respect you will have for the real use for money—to be independent—and the longer your good investments will last you.

Okay, let's see what is needed to get the show on the road . . .

I'm assuming, reader, that you are young and you have a job. If you're older and have been working for some time but have no investments, then the road will require a lot more sacrifice, meaning a higher rate of financial sacrifice.

Regardless of your position, to reach your goal will take

DISCIPLINE—heaps of it!

PLANNING—to achieve a certain goal and then staying focused on this goal.

FINANCIAL SACRIFICE—meaning missing out on a few of the so-called 'niceties' that make life slightly more pleasant.

It is also worth noting and remembering that 82% of parents with high-profile sports kids (Olympians, high achievers, etc.) unintentionally end up in retirement scrimping and saving just to make ends meet.

Paying for years of expensive coaching fees, plus expensive equipment for your kids to maybe *become successful is not planning for retirement.*

Eventually, you are going to have to deal with this scenario. My advice is to let the kids sort themselves out. They will surprise you on how resourceful they are.

Okay, on with the show. The next phase will surprise you.

We do not need to see any financial advisers for financial advice.

Financial advisers do not get rich knowing how to make money. They get their Porsche from the fees they charge YOU. Consequently, the only advice you will get from a financial adviser is that YOU need THEM.

In actual fact, THEY need you.

Financial 'advisers' also include investment managers, real estate people, share market brokers, fund managers, bank managers, hedge fund operators, insurance brokers, accountants—they all make their money from fees, meaning you!

On the very odd occasion that so-called investment advisers get lucky with their guess and actually make profit from an investment using YOUR hard-earned money, they will very quickly take a 20% performance fee plus their 1.5% management fee, and then again, on the other hand, if they cause you to lose money, it's unlikely they will even answer the phone, let alone refund any fees. We definitely don't take any financial advice from someone washing your car or mowing your lawns either!

So the above information narrows the field down to what you do NOT need to do.

So what should we do?

An essential starting point is to work out what investment strategy you'll need that will generate an income stream similar to what you think will be your income at retirement time.

It's definitely not rocket science. A ten-year-old with an iPhone can work it out.

Using round figures, let's say you have decided that $60,000 per year income will give you both a nice lifestyle in retirement.

That's the first hurdle—agreeing on a retirement income amount. Mind you, it should be achievable.

Our ten-year-old then tells us that $600,000 invested for 12 months, say at 10%, will definitely give you the lifestyle you want, that is $60,000 per year, or $1.2 million invested at 5% will also give you the same lifestyle you want—$60,000 as well.

Of course, the problem here is NOT the 5 or 10% return—it's the $600,000 needed for the investment.

How do we accumulate $600,000. The good news is we don't have to have that amount until we are actually ready to retire.

The bad news is that to achieve this $600,000 investment is going to take all your working life plus a lot of discipline and a lot of sacrifice. But even more daunting is it will take an honest household budget that is planned solely to achieve this target through salary sacrificing and sensible spending and also giving up on a few of the luxuries that your peers constantly tell you are essential to your happiness.

It's at this point that eventually serious decisions need to be made.

BUT fortunately, you do not have to prepare a budget that will require you to save all the $600,000 from your income.

There is help along the way.

But first, let's consider some 'investment' options that people use—totally convinced it's the only way to go!

1. *Take weekly tickets and hope to win the lottery. Forget it, it won't happen!*

2. *Buy an older house, renovate it, and sell it.*

It never fails to amaze me the number of young people who think that by doing this, it's the bees-knees when it comes to making big money.

If your partner is not a known interior decorator, and you're not a builder, and your family does not own a hardware complex, forget this scenario, you won't be successful. There are too many dreamy young couples already doing it with no idea and no experience. Have a look in Bunnings on any Saturday morning!

The very best you can achieve, as against what you're hoping for, after spending two years and every waking minute doing up kitchen and bathrooms, floors and landscaping, and paying stamp duty and loan interest, *plus a selling commission and advertising costs, is to consider yourself very lucky to get back the money you've outlaid!*

You most definitely won't be paid for the countless hours you put into the renovation work.

You'd be far better off working overtime at your day job. At least you'll get paid.

3. *Buy a brand new house?*

Do the maths. Your new pride and joy will increase in value at about the same rate as inflation, about 2% per year. The average interest rate on your home loan will be about 7%. Please explain to me how you are going to get rich with this scenario?

However, there are some people who need to buy a home with a home loan. Making home loan payments is the only discipline they are capable off, so it's just possible, after lots of years, these people might end up with some equity in the property, sort of forced savings.

But you're not in that category.

Actually, this obsession with young Australians to own their own home is just plain crazy.

Owning your own home is definitely yesterday's thinking, but it's constantly perpetrated by real estate gurus (for commissions), mortgage brokers and home loan banks (for commissions and interest), and parents as the best long-term financial deal young people can and will ever make.

Everyone, builders, plumbers, real estate agents, mortgage brokers, banks, advertising people, local government, stamp duty agency—all benefit financially, except the person with the home loan.

Face the facts. Houses are consumables; they are not 'investments' that pay dividends.

Houses, once they are built, are then used up by the occupiers.

On the other hand, investments in, say, manufacturing produce jobs and more jobs as the business grows. And as the business grows, the investment grows.

Imagine if all the money tied up in home loans in Australia was more sensibly invested in companies capable of adding value to our endless amounts of iron ore or our vast reserves of bauxite or copper, nickel, even agricultural raw materials. How self-sufficient would that make Australia!

We also have the best 'wizz kids' in the world who head off overseas because of lack of investments in Australia!

How can that help Australia?

And still pathetic, myopic, vote-seeking governments continue to encourage 'young people' to borrow to buy their first home with all sorts of taxpayer-funded grants and first home-buyer schemes.

Okay, after absorbing all the above info, and maybe deciding not to go into hock and buy a house, is actually easier said than done. The female component of the partnership will definitely have something to say about this decision. You see, young females, not being predisposed towards 'investments', are actually fully expecting to gain a 'nest' from this partnership, hopefully ASAP. Kids and 'nest' are their number one priority.

But in reality, any place with a roof will suit the kids as the kids' priority is to be able to crayon every wall. So for that reason alone, it's best if it's a rental!

However, before you can even get to first base investment-wise, as a couple, you need to get your heads around the folly of this home-buying scenario. And then make a commitment one way or another.

On another note, this is how crazy the government has let the system fall into disrepair. It's easier for a young couple to borrow a million dollars to purchase a grossly-overpriced secondhand house than it is for a person to borrow $300,000 to start a new business, which will employ people.

Does that make sense? Is this good for the country?

Okay, let's do the maths in more detail to see what a dumb investment a home is.

We buy an average-priced (median price) home for $550,000. Part of this price, not shown in the contract, is $16,500 commission to the selling agent. You will also have to pay $16,500 stamp duty. So on day 1, you have paid out $33,000 that has absolutely nothing to do with the quality of the house. Assuming you borrowed the normal home loan amount of $400,000 on interest only for ten years, to reduce monthly payments, with an average interest rate over the loan period of 7%, then over the next ten years, you will have paid to my bank $280,000 in interest. I'm not complaining, but you should be!

If you continue with the loan for a further ten years paying principal and interest, then you will have paid out another $140,000 in interest, making a total non-recoupable outlay, paid to other people, *of $453,000.*

And this $453,000 is money paid AFTER *paying personal tax.*

Your $550,000 home has actually cost you $1,003,000! Without any improvements!

I'll let you join the dots on that scenario!

4. Residential rental property.

The most popular because it seems a no brainer. In actual fact, it's a dead loss investment. Renters, generally, are not interested in caring for your property or being on time with rent payments. Usually, when the renter shoots through, it will require all the rent money *you collected to refurbish the property to make it rentable again. A truthful bottom-line return is around 0%. And that's if you're lucky to have a 'good' tenant.*

Negative gearing the property, losing money solely to reduce personal tax, is just another dead loss exercise, *especially if it's a condominium as there is almost no capital gain— too many new ones being built— plus a zero rental return after expenses, of which there will be plenty!*

Only accountants benefit from your negative gearing. Actually, accountants touted this NG as a great way to avoid paying tax. Get real! If you do not have a taxable income, you're NOT making money—you could actually be losing money.

5. Commercial rental property.

A slightly-better investment as your tenant is generally more business astute. One large million-dollar property, with a national tenant on 8–10% rent return, sounds a no brainer. It is until the tenant does not renew the lease. It could then take up to a year to find a suitable solid tenant—read: NO INCOME—from your empty property. And to add to your stress, there is the distinct possibility that your new tenant's business could fail. About 50% of new businesses do fail.

As for capital gain, if you don't or cannot increase the net rent (e.g., because of competition), then there will be no capital gain as the property value is derived from the amount of net rent contained in the lease contract.

Best to leave your local commercial real estate property to the business experts.

6. Industrial rental property.

Slightly better in some ways. With a million-dollar industrial property, you could end up with five to ten tenants. If one tenant fails, at least you still have some income. The downside is that ten industrial tenants are a lot more careless with your property, maintenance is never ending, collecting rent from all tenants is also time-consuming as they always seem to be on the edge of going broke.

Because there is ALWAYS something that requires attention at your busy industrial property, you can forget about long lazy holidays in the Bahamas. Instead, be prepared for 24/7 property management. Not exactly a retirement plan of caravanning around Australia!

Best to leave it to a professional real estate team.

7. Your own business.

Nothing more rewarding or satisfying than owning your own successful business. However, it's not for everyone. To be successful, your business will require your effort and attention 24/7. You will need a product or service that customers want, and you will have to outsmart your opposition, who will be 24/7 trying to take business from you. All the money you do make in the business will have to go back into the business—it has to keep growing just to stay abreast of the market.

One essential goal for you to aim for is to develop a business that is sellable. When it comes time for you to retire, selling your business for a million, or two, will certainly make retirement a lot more pleasant. The downside is that there is an element of serious risk. Your business could fail. This would be an absolute disaster if the business goes bust close to retirement. Plus, a 'good idea' does not necessarily equate to a successful business.

Best to think twice before taking the plunge.

Okay, we are now aware of the more dubious ideas of making money, so where to from here?

Well, for a start, we will need a place to live, so . . .

To the old school, mention that you are considering renting a nice place to live in, and they'll throw their hands up in horror at such an obvious waste of money, dead money, they call it.

But the same old school don't seem to think paying loan interest on a house is dead money?

Trust me, both outgoings are dead money.

But having made a decision that buying houses is not the brightest financial idea, and because we have to live somewhere, renting is really the only sensible option.

For young people just starting out for work, and being broke from educating oneself, nothing comes cheaper than living with Mum and

Dad. Stay there as long as possible, save as much as possible, so when you do get kicked out, which will happen, you'll be able to stand on your own two feet and pay rent.

Tell me again, what's so sensible about renting?

When you BUY a house, all saving discipline disappears. All spare cash now goes into improving the perfectly-good house, paying rates, paying insurance, paying interest, doing maintenance, or out of boredom, changing things that don't need changing, buying new plants, installing solar panels, installing a swimming pool, bar room, bigger plasma screen, pergolas, alfresco areas—spending on totally unnecessary things, spending that's taking you further from the goal of a comfortable retirement.

When you rent, you do not waste or spend spare cash on someone else's property. The property owner (landlord) now does all the above for you—pays the maintenance, pays the rates, pays the insurance—all at their expense! Sure you pay rent, but the rent you pay is always less than the interest payments you would be paying if you owned the property.

With no desire to improve the rental property, no rates, no insurance, no maintenance, no interest to pay, we are finally in a position to actually have cash to start investing.

So absorbing all the above and now being, hopefully, fully aware of all the useless but popular so-called investments that lazy investors get tangled up in, we should now be in a position and frame of mind to start looking outside the square, a place where young people have never been and a place where elderly people fear to tread.

Curious?

Then the following rental situation should be of interest to you.

I recently rented a very charming cottage-style beach-side house from an elderly couple who had paid $750,000 for the property. They were still working in another city, trying to pay off this investment. The agent charged me rent of $350 per week ($18,200 per year).

Whilst I was enjoying the beach lifestyle, I invested the same amount as what the property cost the landlord ($750,000) in a blue-chip company that was paying 11% dividends. The owners of the property collected $18,200 per year from me, less their 'outgoings' (rates, insurance etc.), and I collected $82,500 per year in dividends for the same outlay.

Welcome to the share market and blue-chip companies.

I can totally understand if your first reaction, like the majority of the population to the 'share market scenario', is it's a scary place where people lose their money!

You are partially right—most buy wrong; maybe 'misguided' is a better word. If you buy the wrong shares, or if you borrow money to buy shares that fall in value, or if you try to 'outsmart' the market by 'playing' the market, you definitely will lose money.

Also, if you have anything to do with ANY of the following, you will lose money.

- *A dubious parcel of 'diversified' shares. Read: no prospects, no dividends.*
- *Exchanged traded funds*
- *Put or call options*
- *Any type of derivatives*

- *Annuities (if you die too soon)*
- *Collateralised debt obligation.*
- *Forex trading*
- *Property investment funds*
- *Foreign equities*
- *Hedge funds*
- *Negative gearing*
- *Arbitrage deals*
- *Hybrids*
- *Gold/silver certificates*
- *Leveraged buyouts*
- *Exploration companies (oil/minerals)*
- *IPOs*
- *Nigerian scams*
- *Cayman Island havens*
- *Crypto currencies*

Or any other hare-brained schemes dreamt up by brokers and financial gurus whose only interest is your money becoming their money.

If somehow you do lose the plot, and find that you now own some incomprehensible shares in any of the above that accidently make money, don't for one minute think you have got the market wired. Your next financial adventure in this fool's world will probably end with your 'face being ripped off'. Read: totally fleeced.

In our case, we will only use the share market for one reason: to purchase the certificates (shares) to be a part owner in Australia's safest, most profitable blue-chip company(ies). But before we venture to the stock exchange, there is work to be done.

The first phase is to decide how much you need in retirement and how much to put aside from your salaries.

We can and should review this amount quite often, but one thing is for sure, the amount saved and invested each week will definitely have a serious bearing on the lifestyle you will experience when you do retire. The more you put aside today, the more you can spend in retirement, or the sooner you can retire!

However, the amount you decide to set aside for investing should not be a ridiculous amount. It should be sustainable and comfortable, without causing stress or arguments, and it should also be influenced by the amount of time between today and the day of your proposed retirement.

How much then?

It's really a matter of sitting down with a pencil, paper, and calculator. How much income you want in retirement and how much time have you got to achieve this investment amount are good starting points.

For example, let's work on at least having the basic wage of $70,000 per year as a retirement income.

Let's assume both of you are around 25-ish and have a reasonable total income. Let's aim for retirement at 65.

That gives us 40 years to get our act together, less if you are older.

Banks in Australia are the safest investments. No question. Being too big to fail, they won't fail. So I'm going to recommend banks because of their reliable dividends as a source of income to get your retirement-fund vehicle on the road.

Any bank will be okay as banks generally pay about a 6–8% dividend relative to their share price.

For example, CBA share price, at time of writing, is around $90. The annual dividend should be around $7, with franking credits added back. (see franking credits chapter)

To end up with $70,000 per year income, you would need to own 10,000 CBA shares, or you might prefer to stay with your own bank, say the ANZ. In that case, you would need to own about 32,000 ANZ shares to still get your $70,000 pa. Remember, this amount includes franking credits.

To accumulate 10,000 CBA shares over 40 years, we would need to buy about 250 shares per year. Fortunately, you won't have to buy all the shares from your salary as, eventually, the dividends will also be available to purchase shares. It gets easier as you get older!

Note: Even in the darkest days of the global financial crisis, the banks still made a profit and paid healthy dividends.

Okay, on with the show.

If you are older than 25, or you wish to retire sooner, or you want more spending money, then you will need to purchase more than 250 shares each year.

Start with how many years until retirement . . .

How much spending money per year do you want during retirement?

How many shares at $7 pa dividend will you need?

How many shares per week (or month) do you need to buy to reach this total shares target?

If your first effort results seem unmanageable or unattainable, then try a longer working life or a lesser retirement spending amount, and do another calculation. Keep in mind that your salary will probably increase, the share price may collapse (excellent buying opportunity), the dividends will increase, you might inherit some money—lots of things can happen, just don't depend on it. There is also help from your employer if you work for someone.

Your employer is obliged to pay into an industry super fund 9.5% of your gross salary.

For instance, say your total salaries are $120,000. Then your employers will pay into your super fund $11,400 per year, less 15% tax.

This amount, over a 40-year working life, could purchase a substantial number of shares. Take this into account when doing your calculations. Also, double-check the above figures as governments change the rules regularly.

Whilst on the subject of superannuation funds, with very little research, it won't take you long to figure out that nearly all industry and commercial super funds are not very efficient. Excessive fees and lacklustre management seem to be the norm.

So whilst an industry superannuation fund is perfect for most employed people, there is another option I think you should consider.

SELF-MANAGED SUPER FUND (SMSF)

The SMSF has the advantage of you *being in control, not a responsibility to be taken lightly, though, as there are strict guidelines.*

But here is the good news: Up to a certain amount, wages put into a SMSF are currently taxed at 15%, which is probably less than your personal tax. Company shares that you select can also be purchased by the SMSF. Capital gains from share sales are also taxed at a very low rate in the SMSF; same with dividends from your share investments, the SMSF is very tax friendly.

Here is even better news: Presently, if you're retired, then all the dividends from shares in your SMSF will be tax free. If your company issues 'franked' dividends, then the taxation office will eventually issue you with a refund of the tax paid by that company. Capital gains from share sales are also tax free. How good is that? It's a no-brainer! But only 3% of retirees have the nous to grab this advantage!

Hopefully, at this point, that is, after being made aware of all the pitfalls and dubious investment strategies that innocent and/or inexperienced young people get talked into by so-called experts, you realize that becoming independent is not 'all work and no play', especially with all the help along the way.

The whole strategy is a lifestyle that leads to a better lifestyle.

Staying focused *is the key!*

FRANKED DIVIDENDS

You would be surprised at how many retirees are totally confused about this aspect of dividends.

Let's have a go at un-confusing the scenario . . .

Most blue-chip companies pay franked dividends. *Some companies also pay partially-franked dividends, and some dividends are unfranked.*

A franked dividend means the issuing company has paid to the ATO 30% company tax, paid from the bank's profits. The dividend the bank pays you is what remains of the profit after the company tax has been paid.

Because, as with most shareholders, you are not required to pay company tax, your accountant will claim back the total 30% tax, and then you will be obliged to pay normal personal tax on the gross (unfranked) dividend, which, in most cases, is considerably less tax than company tax.

If the blue-chip company franked dividend is paid into your SMSF fund prior to your retirement, your accountant will claim back the 30% company paid tax, and your fund will then pay 15% tax on the gross unfranked dividend. A big saving as 15% is usually less than your personal tax.

If the same company pays the franked dividend into your SMSF fund after you have retired, your accountant will then claim back the 30% tax, and no further tax will be payable.

It doesn't get better than that!

Note: If you're curious about a company that pays franked dividends, *and you want to know how much those dividends are worth before they are franked, then multiply the franked dividend by 0.433. then add the answer to the franked dividend. This will give you the* un-franked *dividend amount, which is important to an SMSF investor.*

For example: a $2.50 franked dividend X 0.433 = $ 1.08c

$2.50 plus $1.08c = $3.58c unfranked dividend

WINNERS AND LOSERS

This section of the book MONEY, MONEY, MONEY, *is not an endorsement for you to start thinking that because you 'own' the most successful bank in Australia, you are now a 'hot-shot investor'.*

Get the terms 'hot-shot investor' and 'share trader' totally out of your financial dictionary—it's not for you.

If you've adhered to the previous advice in this book, then you are an 'owner' of a great company that will eventually allow you to live the lifestyle you deserve.

That's all you need to know. End of story.

However, the share market is an interesting place. The stupidity of the 'market' will keep you intrigued for the rest of your days.

There are lots of things about the share market that will take you years to learn, so why not take a shortcut to this information—information that should prevent you from getting tangled up in all the hype and crap perpetrated by vested interests on an hourly basis every day or before the unpredictability of this financial circus sends you crazy.

The first lesson, though not necessarily the most important, is that share prices and the 'all ordinaries' go up, and they go down!

In nearly every case, the ups and downs of the market happens for NO *sensible, logical, rational, or obvious reason at all.*

So the following is the most important lesson you will need to learn about the share market.

It matters not one skeerick how much information you've accumulated about the market or a particular company. Whatever you think will happen WILL NOT HAPPEN or has ALREADY HAPPENED!

YOU are at the very bottom of the food chain when it comes to profitable information, so what you 'know' is really history and useless.

The above is the most important lesson you will learn about the share market.

NO ONE, not rocket scientists, quants, mathematicians, astrophysicists, or mainframe computers can predict what the share market will do at ANY time in the future.

You can GUESS what will happen, and maybe, just maybe, you could be right, but unfortunately, most of your well-informed guesses will definitely be wrong.

Making a dollar one day and losing a dollar the next day is a pointless exercise, maybe entertaining, if you don't lose sleep worrying, but still pointless.

Another important point to remember is that the share price of your beloved company will move for no apparent reason. The share price of CBA for example over the last few years has fluctuated between $40 and $96 without ANY change to the bank's modus operandi.

Knowing what causes these 'extremes' in share prices will help you keep a level head when the whole world has panicked.

I guess it's safe to say that 'share brokers' are a big cause of erratic share prices. The more turmoil in the market, the more people panic and sell, or get greedy and buy. Either way, brokers get fees on each transaction and half their luck! Just don't fall for their disruptive fictitious spiel.

Next major culprit of price disruption would have to be 'short sellers', ballsy half-smart operators who sell heaps of shares in a particular company, hopefully spreading panic and causing the price to 'collapse' so the operators can buy the shares back at a lower price.

The other mob that causes share prices and markets to wildly gyrate are the shonks (nonprofessionals) that operate as equity fund managers. They act like sheep—if one fund manager sells, they all sell. If one buys, they all buy, causing a gross overreaction. Inexperienced hedge fund managers, exchange traded fund managers, insurance companies, investment banks, just to name a few are all just as flighty—that is, they jump and panic at the slightest rumor, selling or buying and causing an overreaction on the market. And these are people playing with the money of other people who should know better.

However, the biggest 'crashes' in the market are caused by investors who have bought the bulk of their portfolio shares using borrowed funds, *provided by their margin loan. Any downward trend in the price of their shares will precipitate a 'margin call' by their financial institution.*

If the investor does not have the cash to satisfy the margin call, he will have to sell shares, causing further deflation of the share price, causing further shares to be sold, and so on. This is exactly the reason for the 2008 global financial meltdown.

This feature alone—that is, borrowing money to purchase shares—is the greatest cause of the market artificially rising and also the greatest cause of the market collapsing, often proving fatal to the borrower.

Don't borrow!

So with all this 'interesting' information, is it possible to make money buying and selling shares on the open market?

The answer is yes with extreme reservation.

In 2008, the global financial crisis caused credit (margin call money, long-term loan money) to literally dry up all over the world. With margin calls being the order of the day, the markets collapsed. Share prices and property went into a nosedive. Shares lost 50% of their value.

CBA were $62 a share before the crash and dropped to $27 after the crash. Nothing had changed at the bank—it was business as usual, and they continued to make a profit. At $27 per share, it was a perfect buying opportunity as the same CBA shares eventually recovered to reach $96.

A 'crash' or buying opportunity like this seems to come along every five to ten years, but it's hard to pin down to a more specific time.

However, there are signs of impending crisis. Remember them all!

When the government is adamant that 'things' are rosy, consider selling.

When your neighbour gives you advice on the 'hot' buys, sell.

When banks encourage you to borrow money to buy shares or loan 99% valuation to buy property, sell.

When the media gives accolades on how well the share market is performing, sell.

When you are bombarded with 'buy' advice from brokers, fund managers, or investment advisers, sell.

When the 'all ordinaries' reach a record high, sell.

You may miss out on some capital gain by inaccurate timing, which you should expect, but if the market eventually plummets, CASH is king, and understand this: The market always recovers, providing healthy capital gains for cashed-up investors who have bought near the bottom of the market.

If you're unsure but suspect the market may drop, sell half your shares. This way, you will still get capital gain if the market keeps rising, and if it does fall, you will have cash to purchase shares at a greatly-reduced price.

Another indicator of change approaching is to keep a close eye on the volume *of shares being traded each day. High volumes generally indicate something is going on. (see final chapter:* Capitalising on Share Anomalies*)*

In a sensible rational world, the share price of a sound blue-chip company is very relative to the gross profit after deducting operating expenses. Generally, the share price is acceptable when it is around 12–14 times the annual profit. (see chapter PE Ratio)

If the share price in a normal market is less than, say, ten times the annual profit, that would indicate a good time to buy. On the other hand, if the share price in a hyped-up market reaches 20–30 times the annual profit, bail out—the shares are overpriced and oversold.

Another 'hint' for getting the most out of the market is if you inherit or, over time, end up with a bunch of useless nonperforming shares, do some research and find a share you think will increase in value, sell all your useless shares, even at a loss, and invest the money in the share with the possible capital gain.

To hold nonperforming shares because selling them will show a loss is pointless.

Finally, being aware of all the above, keep in mind that at the end of the day, you have basically become a part owner in the bank so as to receive dividends, which will be your source of retirement income.

In your case, capital gain is not your main purpose. It's nice to have, but once you have sold a share for capital gain, you can no longer receive dividends.

Finally, DO NOT TRY TO OUTSMART THE MARKET. By owning the bank that supplies credit to the market, you have already proved how smart you are.

DIVERSIFICATION

Sometimes, during long lunches, once the conversation gets around to 'money and investments', which it inevitably does, friends often ask me if they should invest in such and such company or if should they consider a move into resources or energy, etc.

I'm always reluctant to give a 'yes' answer or a 'no' answer to that loaded question.

Instead, I say, 'Do some research on this company or stock, and then you convince me why I should buy this type of stock or company'.

This usually brings the conversation to an abrupt silence. Until the next question. It's then I find out the word 'research' is the word that has precipitated the silence. 'What do you mean by research?'

Basically, it means to find out as much as possible about the target company, then make a decision to get involved or run a mile.

Research is not as easy as it sounds. In the share market investment world, research is done by professionals, nearly always people with a degree in economics, accountancy, physics, or mathematics for instance. They are usually employed by banks and funds as 'analysts'. Their sole responsibility is to dig deep into companies and arrive at a trustworthy opinion of whether the company is on solid ground or is all smoke and mirrors or, worse, 'a house of cards'.

Sometimes analysts get it wrong. Enron, LTCM, Bernie Madoff all come to mind.

So back to the question from my lunch friends, what do I mean by 'research'?

Basically, if you don't know anything about a company, don't invest.

When my friends Warren B, and Charlie Munger decide to invest, they get off their backside and visit the company. They sit down with the owner of the firm or the CEO or the accountant and fire endless questions. If they like who they are talking to, and if they like what they hear, they invest.

So to make a truthful decision about a particular potential investment, what you, as a novice need to know, is what questions Warren and Charlie would ask and need answers to.

Pick any business, and there would be a million questions. But to point you in the right direction, there are basic research questions with answers that will put you well on the way to having reasonable confidence to make an informed decision to invest or not to invest.

But get your head around this: You, as a novice, will never be privy to 'inside information'. You're too far down the information food chain; consequently, if something is presented to you as 'inside info', forget it, and forget the person giving it to you, especially if they are on the receiving end of fees. Trust me, this 'info' will be crap or out of date and totally useless.

The same caution goes for 'info' you read in the finance section of the newsprint or hear from celebrity economists on TV. Wild speculation and/or outrageous profit/capital gains projections are the ONLY news you'll hear. Remember Bondy and Skates? That's what sells.

Join the dots!

Moving on.

The basics of your research should include the following, but nothing is in order of importance. Every bit of information is important.

Look at the company's product. Is it in demand (iPhones for instance)? Can the product saturate the market? Can it be superseded? Is there much opposition? Is production dependent on a limited supply? Is there still room for market expansion.

Look at the company's end of financial year profit and loss statement. For a novice, this is quite difficult. Don't assume anything, get professional help from a trusted accountant. Don't get carried away with the profit—look at the liabilities! Some dubious companies bring forward future profits into this year's statement. Liabilities is the name of the game—NOT good if they exceed the sellable assets or future profits. Keep in mind some companies have loan liabilities that are 'off balance sheet'. Then we need to know if the assets are fairly valued. It's amazing that companies inflate their assets, especially when intellectual property and/or resources and minerals still in the ground are concerned.

Check out the owner or the CEO. Dedicated? Passionate about the product? Honest? Qualified? Or maybe he/she has had 25 positions in the last five years.

This is a hard call as there are not too many Jack Walshes, Alfred Slones, and Bill Boeings Steve Jobs left in the business. However, unfortunately, there are plenty of incompetent CEOs left in the system.

Quarterly reports and shareholders demand for dividends burn out a lot of management or cause good management to go off the rails and cover up losses or negative reports or, worse, borrow to pay dividends.

Information on management is very important as these are the people who, with vision and energy, can take the value of your investment to new highs or, lacking qualifications, over the cliff.

Of course, the bottom line of all this decision making is how much it is going to cost to become an investor. This is your most important consideration. Are the shares accurately priced in relation to the assets and the future prospects of the company?

Are there too many shares on offer or likely to be diluted by options? Who owns most of the voting shares? Are they fully-paid shares? Any attached options? What's their price history? Dividend history?

One bit of advice: Don't let the creative spiel of the company-produced investor prospectus sway your decision. The downside information is always missing.

And don't rely on the Securities Commission to keep you safe. Nor rely on the receivers to get your money back. You're on your own.

All serious questions for you for sure, but to not do your research and ask questions puts you in the category of a gambler or at least a major case of sleepless nights.

Which is NOT what investing is all about.

PE RATIO

Playing around in the share market you will come across this 'PE ratio'.

Any information about a company you may be considering investing in (i.e., buying shares in) is useful but not necessarily 100% reliable. Even information directly from the CEO of your target company can be suspect and should be double-checked.

But the fact remains, the more information you can extract from reasonably-reliable sources (e.g., company balance sheets, etc.), the better the picture of the state of affairs of said company; consequently, the target company becomes less of a gamble and more of a decision to invest based on good judgement.

Doing research then requires you to take on board, amongst other facts and figures, the PE ratio.

Don't worry, there is nothing complicated about a PE ratio. The only question you need to ask yourself is, 'is the PE accurate?'

P = current price of the shares
E = earnings from sales after company running expenses: tax, wages, rents etc.

Basically, as far as you are concerned, the PE ratio describes the ratio between the 'earnings' and the current 'share price'.

For example, if XYZ company has 'earnings' (profit) after expenses of $10 per share, and the share price is $100, then the PE ratio is 10 (100 divided by 10).

If the earnings were only $5 per share, and the share price was still $100, then the PE ratio would be 20 (100 divided by 5).

It's well worth remembering that 'earnings' are not dividends. The company CEO may decide to reinvest some part of earnings into new technology, new premises, bonuses, etc., and then, and only then, the board may decide to pay a dividend to its shareholders.

Earnings are not dividends, but the 'earnings' number does indicate if the company is making money.

And the ratio number (10, 15, 25, etc.) indicates if the ASX share price of the company is low, high, or about right in relation to those earnings.

It may also be worth remembering that the general consensus regarding PE ratios is that a reading below 10 is considered low (buy), and a reading of 20 or more is considered high (sell). A reading of 12–15 is generally acceptable.

But these numbers are not set in concrete. For instance, the current crop of ASX investors don't think that Bega Cheese, with a PE of 8, is low. The same investors think that a PE of 56 is not too high for A2Milk. CBA at 15 is okay apparently.

Makes you wonder about investors!

So in summing up, a PE ratio is only a rough guide to what investors think about a company. A high number could indicate crazy investors OR the company has great potential.

A low number indicates the company is in a spot of bother or the market investors are asleep.

But because you have to start your research somewhere, the PE ration is a good start.

Another issue that needs de-confusing is the ratio of dividends *to the share price.*

In nearly every case, the actual share price is NOT *indicative of the potential future dividend. The daily share price can be quite volatile, but the actual dividend generally remains quite static. In a lot of cases, the dividend is usually the same as last year or even slightly higher, regardless of the prevailing share price.*

Some beginner investors get quite concerned when they see the share price drop, thinking that their dividend will also drop. But that's not necessarily the case.

If the share price is down this year, and the dividend is the same as, say, last year, then the only real change that interests you is the percentage 'return' per share.

A $10 share paying $1 dividend is a 10% return.

The same share at $6 paying the same $1 dividend represents a 16.6% return.

The cheaper the shares, the better the percentage return! Of course, the dearer the shares, the less percentage return!

HANG ON A SECOND...

Do you fully understand what you have just been reading?

Yes?

Summarise the most important points then!

Beginners Guide to Capitalising on Share Market Anomalies

After you have been studying the market for at least a hundred years, a market that goes in every possible direction, totally contrary to your best guesses or calculations, maybe, just maybe, at some point in time, your guesses or best-laid plans may have actually been on the money . . .

Well, congratulations on that event, but the real fact remains: You have not got the market wired. No one has the market wired!

So don't go thinking based on your success, it could be time to bet the farm—time to make the big money . . .

Forget it, or alternately, kiss the farm goodbye!

However, with sensible caution, it is possible to work with the situation prevailing in the market and, hopefully, take financial advantage of a specific anomaly or unusual aspect of the market.

For example, when you think share prices at any moment have a lower value than what they should 'normally' be, or shares prices, because of 'overenthusiasm', are a lot higher than 'normal', then we have two situations that could be profitable.

Any other 'situations' in the market will be far too opaque and/or too fraught with danger for your meagre experience and lack of access to serious information, so we will only stick to the above two market events.

Somewhere on your bank-sponsored SHARE TRADING phone app, you should have assembled your favourite shares into a 'watchlist' column.

When you click on a particular share, CBA or FMG for example, you should see what's happening, market-wise, with that highlighted share.

Four important pieces of information are now at your fingertips.

Besides the latest transaction price, you will see (1) the number of sellers, (2) the number of buyers, (3) the volume of shares for sale, and (4) the volume of shares buyers are hoping to purchase.

If you haven't got the above information, work on getting it.

Now let's take the first case where we could make money.

The share price of a solid blue-chip equity you've been watching is heading south.

Why? It's unlikely you'll know why, not immediately anyway.

But what is important is the volume of sellers *doing the selling each day.*

If it's a much higher volume of sellers, in relation to buyers, than a 'normal' day's trading, then continue to watch, at least until the volume of sellers shows signs of diminishing. It may take a few days for this to happen. When sellers seem to disappear, proceed with caution and BUY slowly. Buy small amounts in each transaction as it's a million to one chance of you picking the bottom of the market. It's quite possible the next day they could be cheaper, so it makes good sense not to spend all your money in one hit.

However, you should try and own the lower-priced shares by the time the sellers have moved on and 'buyers' show signs of moving back into the market. Incidentally, this could be spread out over days, weeks, or months.

When buying equities, it pays to exercise patience as the market always drags the chain when rising. It's certainly a lot slower than when the market decides to crash anyway!

Good luck with the above scenario, and remember this: When shares drop by 50%, the same shares will have to rise by 100% to be back where they started!

The other 'event' where you could make money is when the market price of your solid blue-chip shares is exceptionally HIGH. The exhilaration of this high price will interfere with your cool-headed judgement so be aware! No one likes to 'sell' in what appears to be a rising market, so this scenario is a case of personal discipline and courage.

But the same plan of attack as 'buying' applies. That is, the volume is the key. But this time it's the volume of 'buyers' we are interested in.

If there are a lot more buyers than sellers, day after day, just sit tight. When the volume of buyers starts to diminish, start to consider SELLING. Again, you probably have not picked the top of the market, so proceed slowly, selling small parcels in each transaction, as you could sell at a higher price tomorrow if buyers are still hanging around.

If the 'buyers' start to fade away, then sell in bigger parcels, even if the price starts to drop, as we need to have sold all shares before there are no buyers left, only sellers, which will eventually happen.

High prices attract professional sellers (traders), so you have competition.

Again, when the volume of 'sellers' diminishes, which will, then start to formulate a plan to purchase the shares again, hopefully, at a greatly-reduced price, but don't be greedy. Small profits from sales will still make you rich!

Sometimes it's a good idea to not reinvest your actual profits from sales, unless it's into a very solid blue-chip dividend-paying company.

Nothing hurts more than loosing hard-earned profits!

Keep in mind also that the actual number of shares being traded, bought and sold each day, is a clue to future action. A small number changing hands daily requires casual observation. A large number of shares, more than normal, trading each day, requires your undivided attention!

Okay, those two scenarios above will get you interested. But to be successful, we need to throw more information into the mix.

The number of sellers and buyers is important. But we are only interested in the actual buyers and sellers at the market price or close to the actual market price. Same goes for the number of shares actually changing hands around the current market price or close to the market price.

Buyers and/or sellers offering or bidding ridiculous prices should not be considered.

Buyers hoping to buy more shares than sellers are offering for sale generally indicate a rising share price is probable.

Consequently, sellers hoping to sell a larger number of shares than buyers are willing to buy generally indicates a falling share price.

However, the above guide is not black and white, unfortunately.

There are some days when very few buyers are hoping to buy a lot more shares than what's on offer from sellers, and there are days when very few sellers are hoping to unload shares well in excess of what buyers want.

These two scenarios smack of 'insider trading', meaning they probably know something you don't know, so it's important you are aware of this particular anomaly.

Acting on this information will definitely keep you awake at night, but it could be profitable.

And a check list is essential: number of sellers and buyers hanging around the market price, volume of shares available around the last traded price to be sold or bought, and the ratio of shares to sellers and the ratio of shares to buyers.

You're now armed with the bare essentials; the rest is discipline.

When you buy, set a selling price. When you sell, set a buying-back price, and then stick with your decisions.

Note: You need to own shares for 12 months or longer to qualify for 50% reduction in CGT tax.

Finally, you will learn more lessons about the market when you lose money on a speculative investment than when you make money on an investment.

If you do lose money, it's important to remember the circumstances that made you invest in the first place.

You don't need to make the same mistake next time you invest.

You must be well outside your comfort zone to get the big rewards.

KM

HANG ON A SECOND . . .

Do you fully understand what you have just been reading?

Yes?

Summarise the most important points then!

CAPITAL GAINS TAX IS NOT LOST MONEY.

A lot of mum and dad investors (outside of SMSFs) are reluctant to sell shares at a profit. There are several reasons:

1. *The share price may continue to keep rising.*

2. *The capital gains tax will diminish investment monies.*

3. *They do not know what to do with the money when they've sold.*

4. *They were on holiday and not paying attention to the market's selling opportunity.*

Let's just focus on item 2—that is, paying capital gains tax, which you think will reduce the profit from the sale of the shares.

Let's say you bought 30,000 shares just after the last crash, and you paid $50 per share—a cost of $1.5 million. And today the same shares are now worth $100 each or $3 million in total.

If we sell the 30,000 at $100 each, we will realize a capital gain of $1.5 million.

Presently, 50% of your sale profit is taxable (i.e., $750,000) at your personal rate of tax. In most cases, about 20% would be your taxable assessment overall by the ATO. So 20% of $ 750,000 is $ 150,000, payable to the tax man.

Our $3 million proceeds from the sale have now been reduced by $150,000, which leaves us with $2.85 million to reinvest.

I had $3 million. Now I only got $2.85 million to invest. How can that be a good financial move?

It is, and I'll show you why and how.

Because we sold at the high end of the market, the market will, as usual, start to pull back, so we park the cash in a term deposit and watch the share prices. Maybe, in time, you can buy back the shares at close to the price you originally paid for your shares.

Let's say we are, indeed, able to buy back the shares after the market has bottomed out at $60 per share.

With our $2.85 million, we are now able to purchase 47,500 shares, 17,500 more than what we had before we sold them.

Those extra 17,500 at $60 are worth $1.050 million, and at $63.15 per share, you would have recouped your $150,000 capital gains tax.

If the shares eventually gain even more in value, say, back to the price we sold them at, $100, we would then have $4.75 million in our portfolio.

Compare this amount, $4.75 million, against the pre-sale amount of $3 million. A $1.75 million increase in wealth! Not to mention we now have 17,500 more shares collecting dividends.

Consequently, NOT selling would have been irresponsible.

FOMO – FEAR OF MISSING OUT

The dreaded FOMO! I've left this issue until last because this fear of missing out is definitely going to cause you some angst. And it happens to the best of us.

Just when you're really confident and a totally-bulletproof share trader, dead certain on your selling price or buy price, the market does an unforeseen and unpredictable shift: The market spirals downwards, or the market is inundated with a flood of buyers. You, like every other trader, will struggle to guess where the market's now heading, so uncertainty about your selling or buying price will creep into your best-laid plans.

Or if it's the start of a real global-financial-crisis-type downward spiral, then get ready to experience some real serious uncertainty— and fear! You definitely won't be on your own though. Not being sure when the market will stop its freefall will definitely make you a victim of the markets ruthlessness. Indecision will be your Achilles heel.

Welcome to the dark side.

Bottom line, though, is trading shares requires you to make 'buy and sell' decisions, so if you've now lost confidence in your previously-predicted buy/sell prices, then this is when FOMO takes over your life! This is the time when FOMO makes you lose sleep, causes you to be short-tempered, snappy, silent, unable to think straight.

Because you don't know what the market is doing (Who does?), you'll be hesitant to make a decision, trading-wise.

But not making a decision can be costly. And if you do make a hasty decision, and it's the wrong decision, then that could be even more costly.

So if you're hesitant to make a buy or sell decision per your plan A, you are now a FOMO junkie.

It happens to everyone! This fear of missing out because you might sell too early or you might buy too late is what qualifies you as a FOMO victim. And FOMO can get even more vicious.

Having to decide when to sell in a rising market is the hardest decision. That's when fear of missing out will hit you the hardest.

On the 'buy' side, FOMO is not quite so bad. If the market has taken a really big dive, then shares will appear 'cheap', so it's a bit less stressful buying shares. The sell side is the FOMO side.

However, shares don't go up forever. Don't go down forever either.

As a trader, you will have to decide to sell or buy sometimes. So we need to get this FOMO syndrome out of the equation. Otherwise, you'll never make a decision!

It's simple to tell you how but not so easy to execute.

The first part of the solution is 'research'. Find out what you can about the market situation or the shares we are focused on. Then based on your research, you need to set a future 'sell' price, if the market is rising. Also, you need to set a 'sell' price if the market looks like it may be oversold, which may cause a correction downwards.

There is no hurry to set a buy price unless it's a severe crash.

You will now need to exercise personal discipline *and, eventually, execute the trade at the price you have decided on when the market reaches that price.*

If at the last moment you deviate from your previously-set selling price, like you don't sell hoping for an even higher price or you don't buy hoping for an even lower price, and it turns out to be a wrong decision, you'll kick yourself into a coma! So don't do it.

To not deviate from your original buy/sell numbers is the only cure for the 'fear of missing out' syndrome, so don't deviate. Stay with plan A.

Okay then, I hope the above has been educational. But there is still one more scenario that will make your decision-making a bit more difficult.

Most of us have a built-in sense of responsibility. When it comes to money, we feel we have to do something with it. We feel we should use the money to try to make more money—invest it wisely, so to speak. This urgency to invest can be just as bad as the 'fear of missing out'.

If you have no sensible, well-thought-out plan on what you intend to do with the proceeds of a share sale, there is a tendency to not sell, holding on it instead. This can be fatal. If the market suddenly falters and goes south, you'll kick yourself into a coma again!

Remember this: Money sitting in a savings account waiting for a buying opportunity is not money doing nothing—it's money that is working. It may not earn much interest, and it may be there for a few years, but when a crash arrives, buying opportunities will be right at your fingertips.

That's when you'll make a killing. That's when patience to hold the cash in your savings account really pays off!

Conclusion: Set the buy/sell price and don't deviate, then be patient and wait for the next opportunity. Simple.

IMPORTANT (before you finish)

Ask yourself the following questions:

How much money do I have, either in cash or other stuff (property, shares, cars, etc.)?

Write down this amount on a piece of paper.

Now how much of that money is NOT earning income (such as dividends, interest, capital gains, etc.)?

If it's substantial, ask yourself why isn't it earning income?

Okay, in all of the above information, you now have the basics for successful investing, so, now start saving, then start investing and always stay focused on the end goal – a happy, comfortable and interesting retirement.

www.ingramcontent.com/pod-product-compliance
Lightning Source LLC
Chambersburg PA
CBHW021500210526
45463CB00002B/820